THE FORGE

BIBLE STUDY

Stephen Kendrick and Alex Kendrick

developed with Nic Allen

Lifeway Press · Brentwood, Tennessee

EDITORIAL TEAM

Nic Allen
Writer

Jon Rodda
Art Director

Reid Patton
Senior Editor

Tyler Quillet
Managing Editor

Brett McIntosh
Associate Editor

Joel Polk
Publisher, Small Group Publishing

Stephanie Cross
Assistant Editor

John Paul Basham
Director, Adult Ministry Publishing

Katie Vogel
Assistant Editor

Published by Lifeway Press® • © 2024 Kendrick Brothers, LLC.
All Rights Reserved.

Movie images and photography (Cover, pp. 4, 12, 22, 32, 42, 52):
©2024 AFFIRM Films, Inc. All Rights Reserved.

ISBN 978-1-4300-9387-9 • Item 005847375

Dewey decimal classification: 248.84
Subject headings: CHRISTIAN LIFE \ DISCIPLESHIP
\ JESUS CHRIST–LORDSHIP

Scripture quotations are taken from the Christian Standard Bible®,
Copyright © 2017 by Holman Bible Publishers. Used by permission. Christian
Standard Bible® and CSB® are federally registered trademarks of Holman Bible
Publishers. Scripture quotations marked (NIV) are taken from the Holy Bible,
New International Version®, NIV®. Copyright © 1973, 1978, 1984, 2011 by
Biblica, Inc.® Used by permission of Zondervan. All rights reserved worldwide.
www.zondervan.com The "NIV" and "New International Version" are trademarks
registered in the United States Patent and Trademark Office by Biblica, Inc.®

To order additional copies of this resource, write to Lifeway Resources Customer
Service; 200 Powell Place, Suite 100; Brentwood, TN 37027;
fax 615-251-5933; call toll free 800-458-2772;
order online at lifeway.com; email orderentry@lifeway.com.

Printed in the United States of America

Adult Ministry Publishing • Lifeway Resources • 200 Powell Place,
Suite 100 • Brentwood, TN 37027

CONTENTS

FROM THE KENDRICK BROTHERS • CREATORS OF WAR ROOM, OVERCOMER and COURAGEOUS

CAMERON
ARNETT

PRISCILLA
SHIRER

KAREN
ABERCROMBIE

and introducing
ASPEN
KENNEDY

THE FORGE

WHOEVER WANTS THE NEXT GENERATION THE MOST WILL GET THEM

THEFORGEMOVIE.COM @FORGEMOVIE

THE FORGE MOVIE.COM

EXCLUSIVELY IN THEATERS AUGUST 23

SONY   AFFIRM FILMS

FOR INFORMATION ON ADVANCE BUYOUTS AND GROUP SALES, MAKE REQUESTS AT WWW.SONYPICTURESGROUPSALES.COM.
QUESTIONS? EMAIL: GROUPSALES@SONYPICTURES.COM PHONE: 877-488-4258

ABOUT THE MOVIE

Isaiah Wright has some growing up to do. A year out of high school with no plans for his future, Isaiah is challenged by his single mom and a successful businessman to start charting a better course for his life. Through the prayers of his mother and biblical discipleship from his new mentor, Isaiah begins to discover that God's purpose for his life is so much more than he could hope for or imagine. From the Kendrick brothers, the creators of the number one hit *War Room*, comes *The Forge*, a faith-filled movie with old friends and inspiring twists.

IN THEATERS AUGUST 2024

ABOUT THE AUTHORS

ALEX KENDRICK is an accomplished author, actor, and film director, whose credits include *Facing the Giants*, *Fireproof*, *Courageous*, *War Room*, *Overcomer*, and most recently, *The Forge*. A creative artist with a pastor's heart, Alex speaks internationally on the power of film and the surpassing power of Christ. He and his wife, Christina, have six children.

STEPHEN KENDRICK is a writer, speaker, and film producer with a passion for sharing the truth and love of Jesus among the nations. He produces the Kendrick Brothers' films and has cowritten (with Alex) the New York Times bestsellers *The Love Dare*, *The Resolution for Men*, and *The Battle Plan for Prayer*. Stephen is a frequent speaker on marriage, fatherhood, discipleship, and prayer. He and his wife, Jill, have six children.

NIC ALLEN (Bible study developer) currently serves as the campus pastor of Rolling Hills Community Church in Nashville, Tennessee. He completed his undergraduate work in communications at Appalachian State University, and he holds a master's degree in Christian education from Dallas Baptist University. His heart is to see God's Word come alive in people as they mature in faith and make a difference in the world. He and his wife of over twenty years, Susan, are blessed by two daughters and a son.

INTRODUCTION

What's your favorite book or film series? How about your favorite long-running TV show? Chances are, you connect with at least one character and his or her narrative arc. The best stories offer multiple opportunities to understand various characters and their development. *The Forge* is no exception.

Are you caught in the ever-shifting current of worldly culture with little to no regard for the perfect plan God has for you? Are you an *Isaiah?*

Are you like the earnest parent, channeling every ounce of hope you have into someone you love, eagerly waiting for them to catch a glimpse of the gospel? Are you a *Cynthia?*

Are you the seasoned believer who feels called to leverage your life, including your pain, to invest in someone else's journey? Are you a *Joshua Moore?*

It's quite possible you relate to parts of all of these characters. While the details of Cynthia, the dedicated single mom, and Isaiah, her wayward son, may not be specific to your story, there is an element of care within their little family we can all connect with. While the specifics of the route Mr. Moore took to develop a discipleship community may be different from anything you've experienced, there are important aspects of his leadership that the church has in short supply.

The call to be disciples and to make disciples is the central theme of *The Forge* and this coordinating study. During the five weeks of group gatherings, you'll examine the teachings of Jesus and applications within the early church to build a framework for discipleship. Each session includes a film clip as an on-ramp to study Scripture and examine a specific concept. Accompanying each week of group Bible study are three devotional opportunities for you to continue growing through personal study. Along the way, you'll be challenged to look back at how you have been forged as a disciple, seek new ways to grow, and look forward to making a significant discipleship investment in others in the future.

HOW TO USE THIS STUDY

The Forge Bible Study provides five lessons that can be used for group or personal Bible study. Each lesson contains four elements: Start, Discuss, Engage, and three days of Personal Study. Allow forty-five to sixty minutes for the group sessions.

START. Each study begins with opening discussion questions to introduce the topic and get conversation going. This section sets the tone and frames the conversation.

DISCUSS. This section begins by watching a short clip from *The Forge*, and is followed by a few discussion questions to process the clips and how they apply to our discipleship.

Codes to access five clips from *The Forge* are included with your purchase of this book and can be found on the insert located at the back of this book.

Slow or unreliable internet connection? Your Bible study videos can be downloaded to your device so you can play them offline. Simply download your videos on the Lifeway OnDemand App when you are in a place with strong internet connection. Then, you'll be able to watch your session videos anywhere, any time. Look for the download symbol beside your video.

ENGAGE. This section is the primary focus of each week. Leaders should facilitate the majority of the group session using the verses and questions provided in this section.

PERSONAL STUDY. After attending the group session, members should complete the three days of personal study at home before the next group session. Through this personal study, group members will explore biblical content and application that support the concepts introduced in the movie clips and group discussion.

As you complete the study, you'll be asked to list and pray for others in your life who might benefit from the material, and you'll be encouraged to consider inviting those people God put on your heart to join you in this study. Living life in the gospel means inviting others to know Jesus and find life in Him as well.

SEEING LIKE JESUS

"Go and learn what this means: I desire mercy and not sacrifice. For I didn't come to call the righteous, but sinners."

MATTHEW 9:13

START

▶ **Get to know your group by finishing this sentence:**

If I could sit down and have a conversation with my younger self,
I would want to make sure that he or she knew _____.

How we answer that question can teach us a lot about ourselves. Hindsight is certainly 20/20. At times, we all wish we could go back and tell ourselves what we know now—share words of warning and instruction, or perhaps even encouragement and hope. In some ways, the mentors in our lives are messages from the future. What they share with and speak over us are lessons they've learned and things they likely would have wanted to know and hear when they were in our shoes.

Knowing people further along in life's journey who will share the wisdom of their experience matters. As you continue in this study, you'll be asked to note those people and types of relationships in your life and recall those who have mentored you. You'll be asked to lean into those who are or could be currently mentoring you and asked to consider who you might be able to mentor. Investing in others is like having life-giving conversations with your younger self, as you offer help to someone who is now where you once were.

▶ **Pray and ask God to speak clearly in your time together.**

▶ **WATCH the clip with your group to continue the discussion.**

Reluctantly and irresponsibly looking for a job, Isaiah ventured into Moore Fitness to complete an application. When a chance encounter put him face-to-face with the president of the company, he assumed that his attitude and demeanor had closed the door, only to have the hand of friendship extended instead. Over lunch, Moore asked the young man where he would like to be in five years, followed by three key questions. Mr. Moore offered Isaiah the chance to think about his answers and come back when he was ready to talk again. Isaiah returned with modest answers and encountered another surprise from Mr. Moore.

DISCUSS

▶ **TALK about this week's scene from *The Forge* for a few minutes.**

Briefly describe Isaiah and his approach to life.

What differences do you notice between Isaiah and Mr. Moore?

Why might Mr. Moore, a successful and busy corporate leader, spend his time on a young man like Isaiah, whom he'd never met?

ENGAGE

▶ **READ Matthew 9:9-13.**

Matthew and Jesus were an unlikely pair. Tax collectors were hated in the first century. Jesus's kindness and invitation to Matthew would've been totally unexpected.

> *Why is it so significant that Jesus would interact with Matthew and call him to be His disciple?*

> *Share about a moment when someone saw past your sin or your circumstance and still valued and invested in you.*

Consider Mr. Moore's three questions from the perspective of your younger self. How would you answer those questions from your vantage point today?

> *In what ways do you want to grow in this next year?*

> *What kind of person do you want to be right now?*

> *What do you want people to think when they see you?*

Perhaps the answers to those forward-thinking questions are the same today as when you were young. Maybe they are different. Perhaps you see the way those young adult answers came to fruition in your life or how they needed to change over time so you could develop into who you are today.

This week, in your personal study, you will be invited to see people the way that Jesus does, looking past sin toward possibility. As you move forward, ask God to help the members of your group truly see Him and to help you see and respond to others the way Jesus does.

▶ **PRAY to close your time together.**

WEEK 1 • DAY 1
HOLD THE WHEEL

▶ **Begin today's study by reading the following verse from Psalm 119 and engaging with the subsequent prayer prompt.**

OPEN MY EYES THAT I MAY SEE WONDERFUL THINGS IN YOUR LAW.
PSALM 119:18 NIV

Lord, open my eyes, that I may see the truth of Your Word.
Open my mind, that I may eagerly seek to know You more.
Open my heart, that I may grow in love toward You and others.
Guide my hands and feet, that I may follow Your way.

God's Word and prayer are the most helpful spiritual tools we have to align our hearts with God. The psalms allow us to combine these two pursuits in one place. Psalm 119 is the longest psalm in the Bible and is all about the work of the Lord through the Scriptures. These tools are both featured in *The Forge.*

Prayer aligns our lives with the will of God, allowing us to see Him for who He truly is and see ourselves for all we can be in Christ. Did you see the film *War Room*? In some ways, *The Forge* is a sequel to that film. The character Cynthia, played by Priscilla Shirer, is the identical twin of Elizabeth, the character she portrayed in *War Room*. Elizabeth even makes it into *The Forge* to spend time with her sister. Further, Ms. Clara, played by Karen Abercrombie, is a significant character in both films. When learning of Cynthia's dilemma with her young adult son, Isaiah, Ms. Clara offers sage wisdom:

> *"We can't treat prayer like a spare tire that we only pull out in an emergency; it's the steering wheel that you hold tightly every day, no matter where you are going."*

Do you tend to use prayer primarily for emergencies in life or to maintain daily connection to God? Recall and write about the last time you prayed in crisis.

Now, recall and write about the most significant season of prayer in your life, when you connected daily with God. How does God's delight in you prompt even greater delight in you for Him?

Read Psalm 73. Describe the psalmist's state of mind in verses 2-16.

What happened in verse 17 to change the psalmist's course?

Prayer ushers people into the presence of God. From that place, we can truly see the world for what it is, the enemy for what he is up to, and the Lord and what He has for us. Spend time praying today, asking God to reveal to you His presence, His power, and His purpose.

WEEK 1 • DAY 2
LET HIM SEE

▸ **Read this verse and pray that God would apply its truth to your life.**

BLESSED ARE THE PURE IN HEART, FOR THEY WILL SEE GOD.
MATTHEW 5:8

▸ **Read 2 Kings 6:15-18. Then, answer the following questions.**

In 2 Kings 6, we see that Israel was at war with Aram during the days of the prophet Elisha.

What did Elisha pray when his young servant was overwhelmed by the size of Aram's army?

What did the servant see when his eyes were opened?

What did Elisha ask God for, regarding Aram's army?

It's no coincidence that Elisha asked God to make the servant see and to make the opposing army blind. The truth is, we need others to help us see what's around us and notice the ways God is fighting for us. In many ways, that's the role of a mentor or disciple-maker.

At any given point in our lives, if we are faithfully pursuing God, we are all either Elisha or the servant boy (or Paul or Timothy, for a New Testament example)—someone giving insight to others or someone gaining insight. You are either the one being called and positioned to invest in others or the one on the receiving end of the investment.

If you have seen *The Forge*, you likely have a favorite character, even if it's not necessarily the one you identify with most.

▶ **Read the archetypes from the film below, and engage the questions that follow.**

- Isaiah before meeting Christ: the young person far from God
- Isaiah after meeting Christ: the new believer eager to grow in faith yet facing internal and external challenges
- Cynthia: the mom frustrated by, yet earnest for, the heart of her son
- Mr. Moore: the seasoned believer who has walked closely with Jesus— especially in seasons of pain—and now leverages his life and influence to help others follow Christ

Is there a particular person you resonate with most? Explain.

All of us need each of these people in our lives. Everyone needs a Mr. Moore to receive from and an Isaiah to pour into.

When have you had a "Mr. Moore" make a difference in your life? Perhaps someone is currently making a regular spiritual impact on you. If so, describe that individual's walk with Christ.

What role does the Holy Spirit play in letting us see God?

▶ **Close in prayer, thanking God for all the ways others help you see Him more clearly.**

THOUGH NOT SEEING HIM

► **Read 1 Peter 1:1-9.**

Peter was more than a personal spiritual mentor in the life of the early church. Although he had close companions he discipled personally, he also mentored the masses through his letters. Consider today the writings of theological giants like Charles Spurgeon or Timothy Keller and even living contemporaries like David Platt or Tony Evans. These and so many more have a wide reach when it comes to investing in others.

Peter's writings have spurred people closer to Jesus for over two thousand years. In this passage, the aging apostle wrote to dispersed, even exiled believers who had faced great challenges to their faith in Jesus.

Reflect on the depth of Peter's instructions. How do each of the lines below affirm or alter the ways a person sees God? Log your thoughts in the space provided.

"He has given us new birth" (v. 3).

"You are being guarded by God's power" (v. 5).

"You suffer grief in various trials" (v. 6).

What did Peter mean by saying his audience had not "seen" Jesus?

What did Peter explain a person receives and rejoices over, even without having seen Jesus (vv. 8-9)?

In your own words, what does it mean for a person to see Jesus without literally seeing Jesus?

How have you experienced this personally?

In a very real way, Peter saw the end of the story: He knew the difficulty early believers were facing and would continue to endure, and he saw a gloriously preferred future. Throughout the rest of his letter, we can see that he also knew what it would take for his readers to persist in faith. Each of the characters in *The Forge* walked through internal struggles and faced powerful external pressures. They needed the Word of God, timeless gospel truths, and the community of faith in order to see and follow Jesus. So do we.

▸ **Take a few minutes pray about who God might have you invest in.**

GIVING LIKE JESUS

Everyone should look not to his own interests,
but rather to the interests of others.

PHILIPPIANS 2:4

START

▸ **As you begin, invite anyone in the group to share a meaningful moment from the individual study opportunities you engaged in throughout the week.**

▸ **Next, tackle the following group discussion starter.**

> *Has there been a time in your life when you followed the wrong crowd and ended up on a difficult path because of the company you kept?*

Proverbs 13:20 serves as a lifelong reminder that when people walk with the wise, they become wise. When they walk with fools, however, they suffer consequences. Walking with the wise often provides us the opportunity to learn from someone else's mistakes rather than repeating those same mistakes ourselves.

> *Without exposing too much detail, describe a time when you learned from someone else's challenges. Was it because you simply observed their plights and problems or because they learned their lessons and passed on specific warnings?*

▸ **Pray and ask God to speak clearly in your time together. Tell Him you are ready to receive what He has for you today.**

▶ **WATCH the clip with your group to continue the discussion.**

In many instances, the climax of a faith-based film is the presentation of the gospel and a person's acceptance of Jesus as Savior. The narrative spends a fair amount of time on life before Christ, followed by the specific way a person encountered Christ, leaving little time to show the person learning to follow Him. *The Forge* is different in that regard. Not even halfway through the film, we see the central character hear and receive the gospel. As Mr. Moore presented the gospel, he gave a brief testimony describing his own life before Christ and the way his relationship with Jesus changed him. We then see Isaiah walking through Scripture alone and receiving God's gift of salvation. But this is only the beginning of the story. The film makes it clear that trusting Christ is the first step in a lifelong journey of following Him.

DISCUSS

In the clip, Mr. Moore gave a brief highlight of his life before Christ. How would you sum up your life without Jesus in just a few words or phrases?

As he shared with Isaiah, Mr. Moore also quoted his mom and indicated her influence in his life. Who would you cite as integral in the development of your faith? What about them made such a difference in you?

If you can recall specific words of wisdom or encouragement those people offered, share that with the group.

Mr. Moore also shared and explained a key verse of Scripture. You'll encounter that specific reference again this week in your study. For now, what is a passage that is central to your understanding of the gospel?

ENGAGE

▶ **READ Philippians 2:1-8.**

As a group, sum up the passage in Philippians 2, and name the specific parts of Christ's example that Paul instructed believers to follow.

Note the descriptions of Jesus's humility seen in these verses.

How do we cultivate the same kind of sacrificial humility we see in Christ?

When it comes to living out the character of Christ, humble generosity takes center stage. God humbles the proud and exalts the humble (Luke 14:11) and since Jesus humbled Himself more than anyone, God exalted Him above everyone (Philippians 2:5-9). Selfless, sacrificial love communicates Jesus in a way words alone cannot.

This week, you'll be encouraged to give like Jesus in your relationships and spheres of influence. Pray that the same gospel you've received will be one you'll give your life to, passing it on to others in both words of truth and humility of heart.

▶ **PRAY to close your time together.**

WEEK 2 • DAY 1

HEARING AND HEEDING

▸ **Begin this week by reading the following quote from the film:**

*"We don't just call ourselves Christians. We are devoted,
and we will do anything He tells us to do."*

▸ **Read the conclusion of Jesus's longest recorded discourse,
the Sermon on the Mount, in Matthew 7:24-27.**

Jesus explains that merely hearing His words isn't enough—we must apply
them. Read how His brother, James, summed up this idea:

BUT BE DOERS OF THE WORD AND NOT HEARERS ONLY, DECEIVING YOURSELVES.
JAMES 1:22

Note the specific consequences Jesus and James identified for those who
hear but don't heed.

We don't have to search very far to find people who profess to know and
follow Jesus but look and act nothing like Him. As Isaiah continued to see
and experience a whole different kind of faith in Mr. and Mrs. Moore,
he noticed and appreciated those same Christlike characteristics in his mom,
Cynthia, too.

*As you start this week, take a few minutes to think about some words
or phrases that describe true Christianity. From your perspective, what
does true devotion to Christ look like?*

Take time to look up and read the following verses. List how each one describes or points to Jesus.

Philippians 2:3

Ephesians 2:10

Ephesians 4:15

Romans 12:2

Romans 8:5

1 Corinthians 13:4-7

1 John 4:7-21

Galatians 5:22-23

John 15:10

How do your attitudes, actions, and attributes compare with these descriptions of Jesus?

To live in a way that honors and emulates Christ, we must take in His Word and ask Him to transform every area of our lives by His Spirit. As we do, our characteristics won't necessarily compare with His, but His character will actually be lived out in our lives.

▶ **Close by asking God to shape you more into the image of Jesus.**

WE ALL NEED THE GOSPEL

Perhaps you are engaging this study as an unbeliever, exploring the idea of faith while trying to establish community and experience something new. Those who developed this film and composed this study had you in mind and are praying for you. The gospel is the most important message you can hear. May you see, clearly understand, and accept the good news of Jesus through this time.

Perhaps you are a maturing believer. You consider yourself a work in progress (rightly so). Participation in this study is part of an ongoing effort in your life to cultivate good habits, walk in faith, grow in Christlikeness, and lead others well. You need the gospel, too! May you cherish this good news and never tire of hearing it.

▶ **Read how Paul summed it up:**

> Now I want to make clear for you, brothers and sisters, the gospel I preached to you, which you received, on which you have taken your stand and by which you are being saved, if you hold to the message I preached to you—unless you believed in vain. For I passed on to you as most important what I also received: that Christ died for our sins according to the Scriptures, that he was buried, that he was raised on the third day according to the Scriptures, and that he appeared to Cephas, then to the Twelve. Then he appeared to over five hundred brothers and sisters at one time; most of them are still alive, but some have fallen asleep. Then he appeared to James, then to all the apostles. Last of all, as to one born at the wrong time, he also appeared to me.
>
> **1 CORINTHIANS 15:1-8**

Examine the following phrases. Beside each one, list a reason you consider it to be an important part of the gospel, as Paul described it.

Hold to the message.

Christ died for our sins.

He was buried.

He was raised.

He appeared.

He appeared personally to Paul.

Now, underline the phrase that stands out to you most. Explain below why it stands out to you so much.

Why do we need the gospel? Because of our sin nature. Why must we preach the gospel to ourselves daily? Our sin nature. Why do we need to be surrounded by others for accountability and support and led by more mature believers for instruction and wisdom? Our sin nature.

Admitting you are a sinner in need of forgiveness is the first important step in receiving the gospel. Recognizing and remembering the depths of what you have been saved from and the purpose you have been saved for are crucial steps.

We need the gospel initially to be saved and continually to be sustained.

▶ **Close by articulating the gospel to yourself and thanking God for it.**

A FOUNTAIN, NOT A DRAIN

Have you ever heard the expression, "You make a better door than a window?" Viewers might have recalled quips like this as they heard Mr. Moore share the sage words his mother had offered him:

> *"You need to be more of a fountain than a drain,*
> *and you need to start giving more than you're taking."*

Take a moment to unpack that statement. Write out what it means in your own words.

Consider advice you've been given that you've never been able to forget, like the advice Mr. Moore's mother gave him.

Is there a word or phrase you've kept with you that continues to inspire you, challenge you, or protect you in life?

▶ **Read Galatians 5:13-14:**

> For you were called to be free, brothers and sisters; only
> don't use this freedom as an opportunity for the flesh,
> but serve one another through love. For the whole law is
> fulfilled in one statement: **Love your neighbor as yourself.**

Freedom isn't something to be hoarded or abused but leveraged and used for others. Recall the words of Jesus in Matthew 22. When asked by a teacher of Jewish law to sum up the Old Testament commands and identify that which was primary, Jesus quoted the "Shema" from Deuteronomy 6. He explained that the first and foremost command in Scripture is to love God with everything a person is and has (Deuteronomy 6:5; Matthew 22:34-40). Jesus also offered the second, which He said was like the first. When a person loves God, he or she will also love others.

When a person lives like a fountain, flowing with an attitude of love for others through expressions of service toward others, he or she is living like Jesus. Mr. Moore explained that he had previously used people to reach his own goals without actually loving them at all.

Write down personal examples of when you lived like a drain.

Now, write down practical ways you might be a fountain, and give love like Jesus to those in your family, community, spheres of influence, and beyond (for a clearer image of what it means to be a fountain, see John 7:37-39).

▶ **Ask God to help you be a window for others to see His love and a fountain for it to flow steadily through you.**

LEADING LIKE JESUS

So don't be ashamed of the testimony about our
Lord, or of me his prisoner. Instead, share in suffering
for the gospel, relying on the power of God.

2 TIMOTHY 1:8

START

► **Take time for discussion regarding the personal study sessions.**

What stood out? What hit hard? What stirred in you as you spent time with God this week?

► **Following a brief time of sharing, tackle the following group discussion starter.**

Couch-to-marathon training plans for moderately healthy people vary in suggested length from sixteen to twenty-four weeks. They start small and climb a ladder of endurance toward longer-distance runs as people prepare for the daunting 26.2-mile achievement. It takes hard work and discipline. A person sets a goal, sticks with the plan, and gives it his or her all to complete. Any worthwhile achievement in life takes effort and involves sacrifice. There will always be a cost attached.

Around the group, recall and share about a time when you set a goal and worked toward it over a long period. What were the trade-offs? How hard did you work? What obstacles did you face? Were you successful?

► **Pray and ask God to speak clearly in your time together. Tell Him you are ready to receive what He has for you today.**

▶ **WATCH the clip with your group to continue the discussion.**

The clips from the last session showed Mr. Moore presenting the gospel and Isaiah receiving Christ. In this week's clip, Isaiah shared the good news. Further, Isaiah wanted to know what's next and understood there was much more to following Jesus than only receiving His forgiveness. Beyond receiving salvation, believers are invited to live their lives according to it. Mr. Moore explained that there is a cost. You will spend the better part of this session and your personal study time this week examining this cost. In today's clip, we can see that nothing would deter this eager young believer. Isaiah exclaimed, "He died for me, so how could He not be worth everything?"

DISCUSS

Who taught you "what's next" in following Jesus when you first trusted Him and became a Christian?

Would you say that most of the believers you know understand the cost of following Christ or are more concerned with the benefits rather than the commands? Why?

Mr. Moore communicated the identity of a true follower of Jesus through his words and actions. He didn't perpetuate a false, works-based gospel. He also clarified that Jesus isn't an easy, problem-free path toward prosperity. Do you tend to lean toward one of these faulty perspectives of Christianity? How would you describe the cost of following Jesus?

ENGAGE

▶ **READ 2 Timothy 1:6-14.**

In this passage, Paul was clear that the call on Timothy's life would involve sacrifice and suffering. In the film, Mr. Moore explains in fairly vivid detail (quoting the book of Luke) the sacrificial cost of following Jesus. He even cited a personal example in his own life.

What does this passage indicate about the discipleship/mentoring relationship?

When have you been apart of or observed this kind of relationship?

What are some examples of this type of relationship from the film?

This session is much like a diving board into the pool of understanding Christian leadership. You don't have to dig deep in the gospel to find Jesus talking about and living a life of incredible sacrifice motivated by love. Both Paul and Peter made that a central theme of their teaching and letters as well.

The journey of living out your salvation requires wrestling with and understanding the sacrifice that has been made for you. The journey of discipleship is wrestling with and understanding the sacrifice you are called to make in response.

As you engage in the personal study exercises this week, you will continue to consider this cost. Approach each day with an open heart, praying for clear vision from God. The more you see Christ and His glorious sacrifice for you, the more willing you will be to make any sacrifice He asks of you.

▶ **PRAY to close your time together.**

WEEK 3 • DAY 1
WORTH EVERYTHING

▸ **Welcome to week 3 of your personal study.**

It's common for people to set lofty and often unrealistic goals on January 1 or milestone birthdays. Many pertain to exercise and physical wellness. Personal trainers and fitness experts will tell you that these goals start in the mind, but they can't remain there. Eventually, we have to take practical steps toward those aspirations.

In the film, after trusting Jesus for salvation, Isaiah indicated he knew there was more to life in Christ. In his words, he wanted it all. Mr. Moore was impressed. He explained, "People want salvation—believing in Jesus. But very few people want to follow Him into discipleship."

Isaiah wondered why. Mr. Moore answered, "There is a cost attached to it," and shared Jesus's words from Luke 9:23-27. Matthew's account is a little more detailed.

▸ **Look up and read Matthew 16:13-26. Then, journal your responses to the following questions.**

Why did Jesus make a distinction between His community reputation and the disciples' interpretation of who He was?

Jesus used a different word for rock than he did for Peter when he talked about building the church: "You are Peter" (*petros*—small movable rock); "on this rock" (*petra*—massive immovable rock), "I will build my church" (v. 18). Both Romans 9:33 and 1 Corinthians 10:4 make clear that Christ is the Rock.

There are various interpretations of Jesus's declaration regarding Peter in verses 17-18. Some assume Jesus was referring specifically to Peter and his role in founding and leading the church after Jesus's resurrection and ascension. Some assume Jesus was referencing Peter's confession of faith, meaning the blessing applies to all who make this determination. Either way, to declare Jesus as the Messiah, the Son of the living God, comes with a cost.

What are some examples of the cost of making this declaration today?

Jesus described the cost attached to following Him with the image of the cross. A cross brings about death. What have you had to put to death in your life to more fully know and follow Jesus?

Mr. Moore used the picture of a full plate to illustrate that he had so many other things contending for his attention in life when he became a Christian. So, he gave up golf. Isaiah was surprised to realize God doesn't just call believers to resist sin; He sometimes calls them to eliminate good things that occupy too high a priority in their lives. Isaiah got it:

"He died for me. So, how can He not be worth everything?"

▶ **Spend some time in prayer, asking God to show you anything in your life He might call you to lay down to focus more on Him. Write anything He is teaching you in the space below.**

FOLLOW AS I FOLLOW

▸ **Read 1 Thessalonians 2:1-8.**

In addition to the gospel, what did Paul say he shared with the believers in Thessalonica?

▸ **Read Acts 17:1-9.**

What risk did Paul take when sharing the gospel in Thessalonica?

Considering the relationship between Mr. Moore and Isaiah, it wasn't equally beneficial. Mr. Moore took a chance on Isaiah and offered him a job. He shared personal parts of his life and testimony. He offered early morning time (and even breakfast). He spent time praying for Isaiah and teaching him what it looks like to be a believer and a responsible man. Outside of potentially becoming a reliable employee, Isaiah couldn't offer Mr. Moore much in return. Not only was there a cost for Isaiah as a new disciple, there was a cost for Mr. Moore as a disciple maker as well.

In week one, you were asked to identify a potential Mr. Moore in your life. He or she is an Elisha to you, involved in the process of God opening your eyes. He or she is a Paul to you, articulating the gospel of God and offering his or her own life to you. Consider what personal expense that person incurs because of his or her investment in you.

Make notes regarding the personal costs or assumed sacrifices this leader makes to disciple you in the space below. As followers of Christ, why are these worthwhile sacrifices to make on behalf of others?

Where do you feel led to invest in someone else as a disciple maker— not out of duty or guilt but out of love? Does a specific person come to mind? How can you seize the opportunity and make an investment?

Paul invited the Corinthian believers to follow him as he followed Jesus (1 Corinthians 11:1). He also described himself as a mother in labor, enduring suffering so that Christ could be formed in the Galatians (4:19).

What holds you back from investing in others this way?

Francis Chan notes, "If you wait until all of your own issues are gone before helping others, it will never happen. This is a trap that millions have fallen into, not realizing that our own sanctification happens as we minister to others."[1] Making disciples is part of your own discipleship.

Paul wasn't perfect. He didn't claim to be. He did claim that Christ transformed his life, and he was happy to share this everywhere he went and with anyone he encountered.

Write the names of one or two people you would like to pour into as a disciple maker by sharing God's Word and your life with them.

▶ **Ask God for the opportunity to be with those people soon.**

TAKE OFF AND PUT ON

▸ **Read Colossians 3:1-14.**

Mr. Moore explained to Isaiah that the main priority of a disciple is to cease living to please oneself and live for God instead, being fully devoted to Him. Whatever stands in the way of total devotion must be put to death.

Using Colossians 3 as a word bank, fill in the two columns below.

Everything a disciple must be rid of in life	*Everything the believer is to put on*

According to verse 14, which attribute is to be supreme? Circle that one on your list. Why is that attribute so crucial as we follow Christ?

Consider taking a quick photo of your list and saving it as a background on your phone or uploading it as a screen saver to your computer. Perhaps you can even print it out and put it on your refrigerator door or bathroom mirror where you will see it regularly for a season.

The gospel begins with this truth: **Christ died in the place of sinners.**

Write 1 Timothy 1:15-16 below, then work to memorize this passage.

Discipleship never goes beyond the idea of Jesus in our place. Christ took our rightful place on the cross. Now, His character must take its rightful place on the throne of our lives. Whatever sits in His place must be removed.

What might God be leading you to "take off" in your life?

What might He be leading you to "put on" in its place?

A season of prayer and fasting can reveal these things, as the Lord equips you to be rid of them. Fasting isn't only about what a person abstains from but also what they replace it with. The time and attention given to food is substituted with energy and affection for Jesus. This includes focused time for prayer, Bible study, and worship.

As a spiritual exercise leading up to your next large group gathering, would you consider a fast? What might you fast from (food, a meal, entertainment, scrolling on your phone, etc.)?

▶ **As you close in prayer, ask God to give you His strength to obey whatever He is calling you to do.**

INVESTING LIKE JESUS

Two are better than one because they have a
good reward for their efforts. For if either falls,
his companion can lift him up; but pity the one
who falls without another to lift him up.

ECCLESIASTES 4:9-10

START

▸ **Take time for discussion regarding the personal study sessions. Invite those who are willing to share something God did in their lives or taught them in His Word this week.**

▸ **After a few minutes, engage in the following discussion.**

Do you know what a "forge" is? It's a blazing oven used to melt metal so that it can be strengthened and shaped into something more useful and beautiful.

This study is about the environments and relationships that form disciples. As you think about the spaces where you have grown the most and the relationships that have literally "forged" you, start this week with prayer. Consider allowing several group members to pray as you begin. Remember Ms. Clara's words that prayer isn't a spare tire for emergencies; it's a steering wheel we hold tightly as we follow Jesus.

Let's begin by praying for one another by name. Pray for significant spiritual growth. Pray for Christlike countenance. Pray for healthy discipleship relationships with those who lead you and those you are positioned to lead. Pray for spiritual multiplication and for God's will to be done in and through you.

▸ **Pray and ask God to move in the ways just mentioned.**

▶ **WATCH the clip with your group to continue the discussion.**

This scene shows a meeting of The Forge. This is a powerful illustration for discipleship. Jesus often used parables or illustrations to make points about the kingdom of God. As we read Jesus's teaching and gain insight into its meaning, we are given glimpses into the character of God. Today, many forms of media also use powerful images to convey their ultimate message. The visual aid in today's clip provides a meaningful picture of the heart of the church. What is community? How is it created? What purpose does it serve? How vital is it? This scene with the sword answers those questions powerfully.

DISCUSS

Based on this clip, how would you describe this meeting of men?

Looking around the circle of older mentors and younger men in The Forge, we catch a glimpse of what true community can and should be like in the church. Describe the best experience of community you've seen in the church.

What are some reasons (or maybe excuses) for why this type of community isn't often "forged" or found in the life of the church today. How can we, as a group, be involved in changing that?

ENGAGE

▸ **READ the following verses and note the elements and attributes that God wants to be present in Christian community.**

  Acts 2:42-47

  Galatians 6:1-2

  Hebrews 10:24–25

  Colossians 3:12-14

  1 Corinthians 12:12-26

  What takeaways do you have from these passages regarding community, authenticity, unity, and diversity?

  Which of these seems most challenging to you? Why?

Like any worthwhile endeavor that yields good results, community takes time. It takes risk. It takes investment. As disciples of Jesus walk and grow together, they learn what they can't live without. As Isaiah holds out the sword and begins to burn under the weight of the extended weapon, he experiences the struggle of life alone. When the other men surround him and aid the effort, he learns the value of what he has.

  Once you experience community as God intended, you won't want to live without it. Wherever you go in life, you'll look to invest in others so you can cultivate that kind of thriving discipleship-driven environment. This week, as you engage in personal study, make that your aim. Identify and invest. It will be worth it.

▸ **PRAY to close your time together.**

WHO'S IN YOUR FORGE?

► **In this week's clip, Mr. Moore emphasized Paul's words in Ephesians 6 and the sword of the Spirit—our primary weapon. Read that reference below:**

TAKE THE HELMET OF SALVATION AND THE SWORD OF THE SPIRIT— WHICH IS THE WORD OF GOD.

EPHESIANS 6:17

As Mr. Moore presented Isaiah with the sword, he asked him to hold it out, fully extended. Even the strongest young man would have a limit as to how long they could keep a ten-pound sword straight. As Isaiah worked to hold up the sword, Mr. Moore talked about how it was shaped with intense heat and pressured in a forge.

The point in the clip becomes clearer with every descriptive word Mr. Moore uses. Isaiah acknowledged how heavy the sword was getting. Finally, with just the fingertips of the other men added for support, the weight of the weapon became bearable.

As Mr. Moore explained to Isaiah in the presence of The Forge, many try to walk alone as far as they can, but the process only becomes heavier and harder. However, "God gives strength when we stand together."

Has there been a season of your walk with Jesus where you attempted to go it alone? Describe it below.

Community and multiplication has always been God's plan to propel the gospel to infiltrate every part of a person's life and every corner of the globe.

Who is in your "forge"? Who loves and encourages you, even admonishes you when needed? Who is always there to point you to Jesus, help you hold steady under pressure, and walk beside you into battle? Write those names below and pause to pray for each of them now.

Perhaps you feel the need to grow that group. Maybe there isn't a Mr. Moore currently in your life. Perhaps you can't identify an Isaiah you are currently pouring into. Ask God to help you identify those you hope to add to this circle in the future.

What will be your first step to cultivate this kind of community?

▸ **Read Ecclesiastes 4:9-12.**

How do these metaphors apply to living in community as God intended?

▸ **Ask God to help you identify these types of people in your life, celebrate when you find them, and work hard to walk beside them. You need these people, and they need you.**

FORGED IN FIRE

▶ **Revisit Mr. Moore's statement in this week's clip regarding the creation of the sword.**

"The sword was shaped with intense heat and pressure in a forge."

Think of the most formative experiences in your faith. There are likely a few mountaintops and miraculous blessings in your journey that you still celebrate. Those are surely significant, but it's often trials and turmoil that solidify our faith in and devotion to Jesus.

▶ **Read 1 Peter 1:3-7.**

What did Peter say is the purpose and result of going through various trials for those in Christ?

In the ancient world, money wasn't minted; it was measured. Precious metals would be heated into liquid and carefully poured into molds. Once they were completely set and cooled, the rough edges would be appropriately shaved. Soft coins could be shaved too closely, rendering the weight inaccurate, to cheat one of the parties. In the Greco-Roman world, laws were passed and enforced to restrict these practices to ensure proper weights and measures. The Greek word Peter used that we translate as "tested" or "refined" in our English Bibles means to approve or recognize as genuine after examination.[2] In Athens, men of integrity examined currency and ensured only proper pieces remained in circulation.

Peter explained that a person's worth would be tested and measured along the way. The genuineness of faith is measured in the face of trials. This examination tests the weight of a believer's faith.

The pure metal forged to form the sword held by Isaiah would have been weighed, heated, and molded to accuracy. Then, it would have been carefully examined and tested before use. One wouldn't quite know the success of the product until it was properly held and wielded. Trials forge faith in fire and measure it's genuineness in battle.

How do you typically view the trials of your life? What would be different if you viewed these trials as having a purpose, being used by God to grow you more in relationship with Him?

In James 1:2-4, Jesus's brother offered these words:

> Consider it a great joy, my brothers and sisters,
> whenever you experience various trials, because you
> know that the testing of your faith produces endurance.
> And let endurance have its full effect, so that you
> may be mature and complete, lacking nothing.
>
> **JAMES 1:2-4**

According to James, what is accomplished by the trials we face?

Based on today's study, why can we rejoice during trials? Does this mean we go looking for hardship? What does it mean?

▶ **Ask God to give you a proper perspective on the difficulties you've faced and to equip you for endurance for His sake. Pray that He enables you to rejoice during every trial, knowing His plans for you are good, and to thank Him after the trial for carrying you through it and making you more like Christ.**

THE GAPS OF FAITH

Among the men of The Forge is Isaiah's Uncle Tony—a central character who had a spiritual breakthrough in the film *War Room*. In *The Forge,* Tony was presented as maturing in faith and mentoring other young men. At a small group dinner for Mr. Moore's group of mentors and disciples, Tony shared about a recent struggle in his faith journey.

Through Scripture, the Lord reminded Tony of the importance of faith when gaps exist between our problems and our knowledge and ability to solve them. Read the verse Tony referenced below:

NOW WITHOUT FAITH IT IS IMPOSSIBLE TO PLEASE GOD, SINCE THE ONE WHO DRAWS NEAR TO HIM MUST BELIEVE THAT HE EXISTS AND THAT HE REWARDS THOSE WHO SEEK HIM.

HEBREWS 11:6

Tony reminded the men of The Forge, young and old, why those gaps exist. If they didn't, we wouldn't need faith and might be tempted to take the credit for solving the problems ourselves.

There are many ways the word *invest* can be used during our study. First, discipleship is built on the idea of investing in others, but it also includes the spiritual deposits made in Christlike character development. Each of these is an exercise in faith. Like any other investment, there are unknowns, but we take those steps anyway, trusting God to fill in the gaps. Faith that knows all the answers and possible outcomes simply isn't faith.

▶ **Read the remainder of Hebrews 11 and answer the question below.**

How are you encouraged by the list of figures named in Hebrews 11? How are you challenged?

Each person trusted God and obeyed Him in faith without fully knowing how everything would work out or what would happen along the way. But they obeyed, and they received a reward from God because of their faith.

While all of these people can be remembered for their faith-filled successes, none were perfect examples of godliness. We are reminded by a quote attributed to Ignatius Loyola that "God uses crooked sticks to draw straight lines."

While some might presume they need to be perfect before making a investment in another believer, that simply isn't true. If you "wait" until you are perfectly ready, you'll never start. Walking in faith means investing in faith and trusting God to fill the gaps. It's not about having all the answers but walking in humility, honesty, truth, and love as you live out your faith and mentor others.

What faith "answers" are you looking for right now?

Where is God calling you to trust Him in the gap between your questions and His answers?

How will you begin investing in others in faith, despite what you don't know?

Spiritually mentoring others is not about teaching them to come to you for the answers but teaching them to seek God and His Word daily for what they need. Investing in another believer means exercising faith, walking in love, and trusting God. You have unique yet relatable experiences that others could benefit from greatly. God can use all of your experiences to influence someone else for His kingdom—whether you feel ready or not. Don't be afraid of the gaps.

▶ **As you close out this week, consider the experiences you've had, challenges you've faced, and hurts you've endured.**

SENDING LIKE JESUS

"Go, therefore, and make disciples of all nations, baptizing them in the name of the Father and of the Son and of the Holy Spirit, teaching them to observe everything I have commanded you. And remember, I am with you always, to the end of the age."

MATTHEW 28:19-20

START

▶ **Take time for discussion regarding the personal study sessions. After a few minutes of conversation, engage in the following discussion.**

What is your favorite inspirational movie scene of all time? A big battle scene? An emotional speech? A great loss?

How did that moment inspire you? Share these favorite movie moments with one another.

Maybe you also have a favorite scene from *The Forge*. If you've only seen the clips featured in this study, you may have a favorite of the ones you have viewed thus far. Our clip for this session is another powerful scene from the film.

▶ **Pray and ask God to speak clearly in your time together.**

▸ **WATCH the clip with your group to continue the discussion.**

Isaiah progressed through a process of discipleship, and we see a variety of men from The Forge investing in him. This montage culminated with Isaiah taking what was invested into him and reinvesting it in others. This is a mission and the goal of discipleship. All disciples are sent by Jesus.

DISCUSS

We don't just call ourselves Christians. We are devoted to Jesus, and we will do anything He tells us to do. Anything else means we're lukewarm. Jesus wants us to be fully devoted to Him. What threatens to keep a believer in a lukewarm state?

Continuing that thought, what propels a believer, like Mr. Moore, to devotion?

As you reflect on the many times throughout this study you've been asked to identify disciple makers in your life, as well as people you might disciple and principles or experiences you might share, what is your next step as a disciple today?

ENGAGE

Throughout the Old Testament, when presented with the choice to believe in God or fear the world, the people of Israel often chose the latter. Perhaps that is not much different than the lukewarm state of many believers today.

What might people fear when it comes to complete devotion to Jesus and total willingness to go wherever He calls and do whatever He says?

▶ **READ Matthew 28:18-20 and Acts 1:8 together.**

These are some of the final words recorded in Jesus's time on earth. After these final words, Jesus ascended to the Father. Central to both of these recordings of Jesus's final words is the idea of power and authority. Jesus has all authority and commands His disciples to go and make disciples. The Holy Spirit gives us His power that makes this possible.

How do Jesus's promises to be present and to give us power help eliminate any fear we have about seeking to make disciples?

The world and the devil will always tell us that it is a bad idea to share our faith or that we don't really have permission to share our faith with others or train others to follow Christ. The One with all authority does not just give us permission but commands us to do so. You have both the power and authority of God backing you up as you advance His kingdom and pour into others. Let's commit to this together.

What is your most significant takeaway from this study?

▶ **PRAY and ask the Lord to help each of you give the rest of your life in service to Jesus, following Him as His disciple, and pouring into others so that they will know and follow Him as well.**

FREELY GIVE

▶ **As you start today, consider taking a minute to look back through your previous group and personal studies. Review the notes you took and words or phrases you might have underlined along the way.**

Is there anything that sticks out to you as primarily important? Write that here.

Is there a particular verse or passage that stands out that you want to revisit? Why?

The primary theme of this study has been mentoring. This takes two forms in the life of a believer: Each of us *needs* a mentor, and each of us can *be* a mentor. Each of these are foundational for discipleship.

▶ **Read Matthew 10:1-8.**

What does it mean that Jesus sent His disciples out with authority?

*How can believers operate under the authority of God?
What does that authority provide?*

*What are some ways we might misunderstand God's authority
or attempt to use it for the wrong reasons?*

Focus on the final phrase in verse 8 and fill it in below.

"Freely you _____, freely _____."

This is the crux of discipleship. As a believer who has received grace and
forgiveness, love and truth, wisdom and encouragement, you are to be
a leader who points others to those same blessings. Because you have
received freely from Jesus and through the investment of other disciple
makers in your life, you can freely give to others.

*As you close today, write a prayer of commitment below. Express your
willingness to live as Jesus's representative and to make disciples
wherever He leads you.*

OVERFLOW
TO OTHERS

Experience doesn't necessarily provide wisdom or maturity. And maturity doesn't always naturally result in sharing with others. Gaining maturity and sharing wisdom require an intentionality that many avoid.

*Make a list of reasons why a person might not use his
or her experience to mentor others.*

Underline any of the above reasons that apply in your life.

▶ **Read Romans 15:13-14:**

> Now may the God of hope fill
> you with all joy and peace as you
> believe so that you may overflow
> with hope by the power of the Holy
> Spirit. My brothers and sisters,
> I myself am convinced about you that you also
> are full of goodness, filled with all knowledge,
> and able to instruct one another.
>
> **ROMANS 15:13-14**

According to this passage, what are you to overflow with, and what is the source of this abundance?

Would you describe your life as overflowing with the hope of Jesus? Why or why not?

Based on your experience with Jesus, what can you share with and invest into others? Make a brief list below.

Near the end of the film, the men of The Forge gathered together, and Mr. Moore asked Isaiah to share. Here is a recap of what Isaiah said:

- He had been meeting with the group for over a year.
- He needed godly men to challenge him and keep him accountable.
- He needed their help to study the Word.
- He needed them to pray for him and with him.
- He felt ready to do this for someone else and was asking God to show him who.

Isaiah was by no means fully mature or complete. He was a work in progress, but according to Mr. Moore and the apostle Paul, he was able.

▶ **As you close this session and prepare to close out this study, let Paul's words wash over you. With God-sized hope, fueled by the Holy Spirit's power, you can instruct others.**

WEEK 5 • DAY 3
TAKE THE JOURNEY

You've made it to the last day of personal study. Hopefully, your life as a disciple has been impacted by this journey. At the beginning of his final words to The Forge, Isaiah made an ordinary but important statement:

"I've been a part of this group for a little over a year now."

Discipleship isn't a one-time event. It is a lifelong journey. Think back to the scene at the start of the movie when a younger Isaiah met Mr. Moore for the first time. Remember the chip on his shoulder, the disrespectful tone in his voice, and the lack of passion in his life? Mr. Moore knew one lunch or a single study wasn't going to upend that young man's life and set him completely on another course. When he offered Isaiah a job and the chance to meet with him before his shift, he was offering a marathon, not a sprint.

Over the last several weeks, you have sought to see God and see others like Jesus does. You have been challenged to give what you have received to others with humility, like Jesus. You have been encouraged to lead and invest in others, not out of your own perfect wisdom but from the overflowing well of hope offered by the Holy Spirit. Now, you are being sent in that power. This isn't a short-term mission trip. It's not a weekend event. It's a life of service and sacrifice.

Conclude your time in this study thinking about the words Mr. Moore used to challenge the group toward a life of discipleship:

"Most churches are trying to win converts, but
not enough are effectively discipling them."

He knew the group needed to expand. He recognized the need to answer Christ's Great Commission to go and make disciples. This is the call of every believer in Jesus Christ.

"Go, therefore, and make disciples of all nations,
baptizing them in the name of the Father and of the
Son and of the Holy Spirit, teaching them to observe
everything I have commanded you. And remember,
I am with you always, to the end of the age."

MATTHEW 28:19-20

Remember that going, making disciples, baptizing, and teaching is a long journey. It will not be without challenges, but you can do it by the power and presence of the Holy Spirit.

After some time had passed, Paul said to Barnabas,
"Let's go back and visit the brothers and sisters
in every town where we have preached the word
of the Lord and see how they're doing."

ACTS 15:36

Paul's words remind us that discipleship doesn't necessarily mean just a season of life spent with another believer. It may include a lifetime of follow-up, connection, and fellowship.

In what ways are you committing to the Great Commission?

How are you partnering with Jesus and with others to fulfill it?

Whatever seasons of discipleship await you, don't hold back. God is with you and will give you what you need. It's time to take the journey.

END NOTES

1. Francis Chan, *Multiply: Disciples Making Disciples* (Colorado Springs: David C. Cook, 2012), 56.

2. James Strong, *A Concise Dictionary of the Words in the Greek Testament and The Hebrew Bible* (Bellingham, WA: Logos Bible Software, 2009), 24.

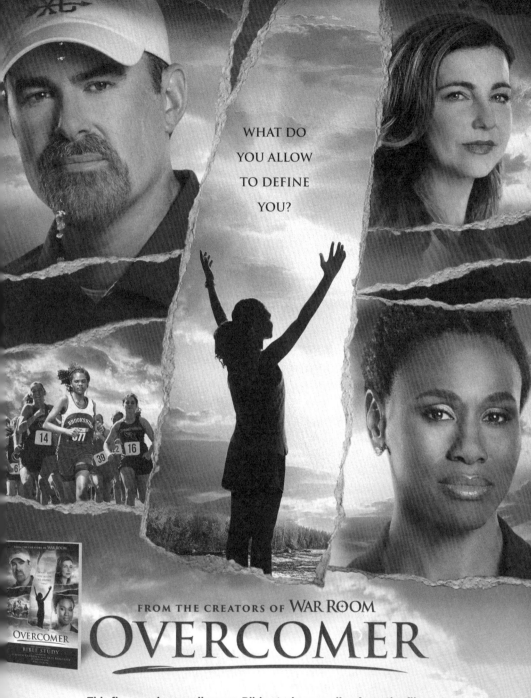

WHAT DO
YOU ALLOW
TO DEFINE
YOU?

FROM THE CREATORS OF WAR ROOM

OVERCOMER

This five-session small group Bible study uses clips from the film
OVERCOMER to examine how we determine our identity
and how we can find our true identity in Christ.

Learn more about this Bible study at lifeway.com/overcomerbiblestudy and
more about the *OVERCOMER* movie and products at lifeway.com/overcomer.

Lifeway

STUDY WITH THE WHOLE FAMILY

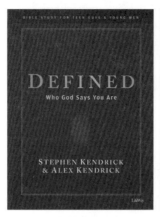

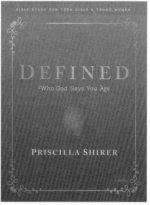

Guys Bible Study Book
005815893 $14.99

Guys Leader Kit
005815899 $59.99

Girls Bible Study Book
005815892 $14.99

Girls Leader Kit
005815895 $59.99

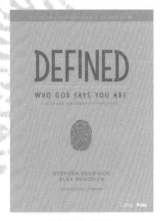

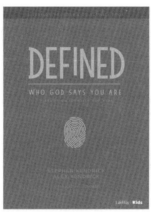

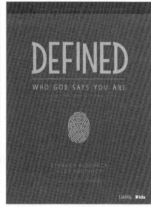

Kids Leader Guide
005814776 $14.99

Younger Kids Activity Book
005814773 $6.99

Older Kids Activity Book
005814775 $6.99

"Who am I?" Someone or something is attempting to answer the question for us. But to accurately answer this question, we must first ask, "Who does God say I am?" The Bible tells us that we are each made in God's image, but that image has become distorted by sin. The only way to restore what was broken is through a relationship with Jesus. These eight-session Bible studies for teen girls, guys, and kids examine spiritual truths found in the Book of Ephesians to address the topic of identity.

Lifeway

lifeway.com/defined

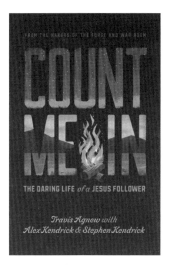
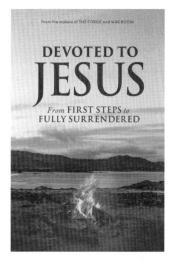

What the world needs now

We don't need another strategy; we need men and women who are devoted to Jesus and lifelong discipleship.

The Forge movie and this Bible study present a simple, reproducible approach to discipleship that can be embraced by all Christians. In this study you'll learn to:

• Pursue Jesus with other believers in community

• Find grace, forgiveness, prayer, and accountability

• Recognize the cost of following Jesus and be inspired to release anything keeping you from fully surrendering to Christ

LEADING A GROUP?
Each group member will need *The Forge Bible Study Book*, which includes video access. This gives participants personal access to all of the video content.

STUDYING ON YOUR OWN?
To enrich your study experience, be sure to access the videos available through the redemption code printed in this Bible Study Book.

ADDITIONAL RESOURCES

eBOOK
Includes the content of this printed book but offers the convenience and flexibility that come with mobile technology.

005849651 $17.99

More resources can be found online at lifeway.com/theforge

Price and availability subject to change without notice.

THE FORGE

Here's Your Video Access

To stream the Bible study teaching videos, follow these steps:

1. Go to my.lifeway.com/redeem and register or log in to your Lifeway account.

2. Enter this redemption code to gain access to your individual-use video license:

79FRMRTVNG76

Once you've entered your personal redemption code, stream the Bible study teaching videos any time from your Digital Library page on my.lifeway.com or watch them via the Lifeway On Demand app on a compatible TV or mobile device via your Lifeway account. No need to enter your code more than once! To watch your streaming videos, just log in to your Lifeway account at my.lifeway.com or watch using the Lifeway On Demand app.

Slow or unreliable internet connection? Videos can be downloaded to your device so you can play them offline. Simply download your videos on the Lifeway On Demand App when you are in a place with strong internet connection. Then, you'll be able to watch your session videos anywhere, any time. Look for the download symbol beside your video.

QUESTIONS? WE HAVE ANSWERS!
Visit support.lifeway.com and search "Video Redemption Code" or
"Video Streaming FAQ" or call our Tech Support Team at 866.627.8553.